The Alchemy of Happiness

Also by Marilyn Bowering

Poetry

The Liberation of Newfoundland (1973)
One Who Became Lost (1976)
The Killing Room (1977)
Sleeping with Lambs (1980)
Giving Back Diamonds (1982)
The Sunday Before Winter: New and Selected Poetry (1984)
Anyone Can See I Love You (1987)
Grandfather Was a Soldier (1987)
Calling All the World: Laika and Folchakov 1957 (1989)
Love as It Is (1993)
Autobiography (1996)
Human Bodies: New and Selected Poems 1987–1999 (1999)

Fiction

The Visitors Have All Returned (1979)
To All Appearances a Lady (1989)
Visible Worlds (1997)

The Alchemy of Happiness

poems by

Marilyn Bowering

Porcepic Books
an imprint of

Beach Holme Publishing
Vancouver

This book is published by Beach Holme Publishing, 226–2040 West 12th Avenue, Vancouver, B.C. V6J 2G2. *www.beachholme.bc.ca.* This is a Porcepic Book.

The publisher gratefully acknowledges the financial support of the Canada Council for the Arts and of the British Columbia Arts Council. The publisher also acknowledges the financial assistance received from the Government of Canada through the Book Publishing Industry Development Program (BPIDP) for its publishing activities.

Editor: Michael Carroll
Design and Production: Jen Hamilton
Cover art: *Almudena de la Peña* by Mercedes Carbonell. Oil on infografía. Copyright © 2002. Used with permission.
Author Photograph: Tony Bounsall Photo-Design

Printed and bound in Canada by Marc Veilleux Imprimeur

National Library of Canada Cataloguing in Publication

Bowering, Marilyn, 1949-
   The alchemy of happiness/Marilyn Bowering.

   Poems.
   "A porcépic book."
   ISBN 0-88878-435-X

   I. Title.
PS8553.O9A42 2003   C811'.54   C2002-911090-4
PR9199.3.B635A42 2003

For Michael and Xan
and for my brother, David

Contents

The faculties rejoice without knowing how they rejoice, the soul is enkindled in love without understanding how it loves.
—St. Teresa of Avila, *Complete Works*

I

The Father and Mother Poems,
The Daughter Poems

The Father and Mother Poems
for David

1. Father

Robin, who is dead, says I should write poems,
I should write about my father,
who is old,
just like he wrote about his father…

A poet writes when looking at death:
a poet sees the crusted mouth,
skin like a slaked wall,
the knobs and veins of dear hands.

The poet sees that age is poverty,
and at the same time, feels the roistering breath
close to the heart of time.

My father lifts me, a baby, from the floor,
he sings in the kitchen making breakfast,
he fetches me home from my broken-down car,
he fills the cauldron of my failed heart with his love—

today I looked into his eyes
and he thanked *me*.

A poet would write his rage,
not talk to the dead at night,
a poet would understand the great gift
of being loved

for so long
so well,

and drink deep,
salute the ghosts, elbow aside a place for himself in bed
next to his dad.

2. Mother

i. Where are the horses
on our night ride?

Through the wall
of golden shower.

I can follow you to the hill
but no farther.

Grief supports me
to the other world,
but the distance draws you.

Remember me:
the well of your love
is my water.

I was a fool to think
I could keep you.

Foolish love.

ii. In the beginning
we set out together.

Now somehow, somewhere,
you've sighted shore.

As for me, I'm still looking, sun-blinded, moon-crazed,

through the lens of wet eyes.

iii. Twelve herons
long sea grass
rocky foreshore
sea wrack
wild roses
broom
swallows
geese swimming
a path underfoot
the silk sea
a boat close to shore

a stick thrown
sun on the marsh
three more herons
still as dried insects

3. A woman walked around the dining table

this morning,
a small boy climbed up,

and I'm worried
he might fall.

Her face wears an expression
stamped there, my father says,
as of *days of yore*

when the first face was made
and its look was fixed
by the maker.

I'm glad it's not you, this ghost who has
returned to circle the table—
you have better things to do—

(the boat in which you travel
has caught a wind,
your hand is cool where it trails in water—
you're almost home!)

Every child loses its mother, I suppose,
the lamp lit from birth goes out,
the child knows the dark.

You are still my light,
and I'll find you
wherever you are.

Now I see why the woman has come—
to show me how it's done.

4. In the house on Torquay, Herbert had a dream:

he saw a green roadster, and his two friends;
the car slid past the window, dressed in clouds;

his friends wore suits and waved.
They called, "Herbert rise up. Awake. Today
is your wedding."

Herbert slid out of bed: his eyes were crescents,
his heart was iron,
a sword had passed through him.

"Wake up!" Behind the mist—a house of storm clouds,
a bridge. "Awake, awake, get in!"

Herbert stood in the dark: the dream swirled
through his head like the woman (even now)
opening drawers, lifting his clothing to her face,

a woman he had once known, her damp, scented skin
on his hands, holding him.

The Daughter Poems

1. I have no dress or shoes,

no book beside the bed,
no dog for comfort,
no house,
just the bed.

It is wide enough,
but is still as a hillside
where cows stalk downward
to a salt lick.

I hold you as if you were a glass
given to me to drink
and to keep safely full,
I hold you as if we are inside
a green tent.

Your eyes are lost buttons
uncovering.

2. The Yellow Dress

It is the kind of dress I can draw—
buttoned,
three-quarter-sleeved,
the skirt a bell,
a floral overskirt—

not something I would buy,
but it suits
the girl with honey hair
who wants the dress.

She opens her mouth—
a note like a charm, a silver salmon,
a shard of glass…

What would make her happy,
is this dress—

put it on, for God's sake!

Grass springs between her fingertips.

3. On the Island of Paros

I wished, above all,
to be a poet,
and I wished to feel
like Archilochus, that old soldier
eating bread on his spear,
that *nothing is unexpected*
or can be declared impossible—so do not be
surprised if the dolphins find the mountains
delightful...

I watched the dolphins swim,
the blue sky, cloudless, like an unwritten song,

and I felt the shadow of the years,
heard a footfall
like a stone
dislodged
by the wind.

Was it you,
and I was being remade
even then?

Love Poem for My Daughter

for Xan at fourteen

You are all the light in the world
gathered into a face,
your eyes deep space and stars—
who are you?

When you sleep, your breath stirs
the brooms of ages, dust shifts:
your skin is gold,
the past opens itself to your many dresses,

the night unravels its blue wool:
you stand on a far shore
about to set sail—
where are you going?

When you laugh,
the graves open, the dead put on makeup,
the souls of children wake up:
who will go in your company?

You are a stir of wind,
the scent of rare wood,
your mind mirrors the breath of sages,
your thoughts are new.

I called you and you came.
I loved you and you grew,
but who knew
this grace,
the wound flower in the heart's chain?

II

The Alchemy of Happiness

Concerning Self-Examination
and the Recollection of God

Self-Examination

You came into this world for one purpose,
and that was to learn
the story of all beings,

but you let the account fade.
You could have asked—they were willing to tell all—
but every hour you neglected dreams
and accumulated regret.

For the whole of your life
you said one thing:
please show me the love in which I reside—
and one day,
in the presence of death,
you saw.

Ah, me.

Shadrach

Sometimes the god
is hanging up laundry
next to a furnace.

He nods, opens the furnace door,
beckons, steps in.

You know who he is,
and his two friends—

sometimes they wash themselves in flames,
sometimes I am washed too,
my skin crisp like gold foil,

sometimes that's all there is:
just the walking,
and the heart still human, exultant—
for something has been understood
about the flame inside, the flame out,
about thought polished to a
molecule-loosening dagger
that permits all.

Meshack

Sometimes the god watches soap
and water slosh behind glass at a laundromat:
not even he can see who or what
is being cleansed—

he waits, like anyone would,
for an outcome
so he can start over
if he has to, or find some other reason

to link inner and outer,
self and self.

Abednego

No gods are visible,
but people buy groceries,
open and shut car doors beneath
unconscious rain from over the sea.

They are well within the view from my father's window
where he sits in a chair
to watch a tree yield, light bend, the horizon
flex as darkness tidies itself
into a sharp drumroll.

I mail my letters,
pray he has time to catch that last
glint
of a mast.

Sooner or later I will try
to name that ship.

The Ship

You can choose what form the flame takes

just as I
chose the stone of your white forehead
on which to place my lips,
and that stone, now, entombs me.

I kept from you
my adoration, my passion,

and that you had my heart all along.
A broken cup.

So it is said, so I know
no one enters Heaven
without their father and mother,

some mending,
some rolling away of stones.

North

If the word for a ship means
glacier, even iceberg,

then there are limits to the world:
seven seas slip between
the known world
and its warm shadows,
opposites crack
the planet.

In the Earth's core—
the fiery furnace.
Inside it, fierce gods
trim their nails,
shape-shift through the hours
it takes to forge a
single silver bangle.

West

Gold straw spikes through
the snow; the horizon
is the next lip of road.

A ball of fire in the sky,
buffalo bones and blue light
in the coulee:

once all the keys are turned
in the lock,
the mountains thin,
the sky tunes itself
to the eye.

All this a gift.

I was not hurt,
just dragging a wing
to lure evil away.

Death

In your heart is a window,
and a furnace in which gods walk, unharmed:
do not accept my word,
follow no one.

The effect of death
is on the heart:

a lamp goes out,
the soul is dismounted.

Don't listen to me,
don't run to it.

It sets off *and* abides.

No vision is necessary,
death is a bridge:

mirror its spaciousness
in the dark wood.

Dark Wood

Hostile to the traveller.

Southeast

Look there: your mother's hands,
and a latch to reach her;

she understands desire:
how she longed for you.

Longing is a match,
heart with heart.

Look there: a woman and child
draw on the glass I mentioned
(shut or open, broken

or whole)—
snowflake
sun
moon
tree house smoke
fire fire fire

Gold stars on the leaves.

Who?

Someone tells you about serpents
and angels and your heart says:
three friends, a fiery furnace, a stairway,
garden, wood, flight...

Who do you think you are—Dante?

Oh, doubt and mystery. The gods
wash sweaters,
pair socks,
complete the divine between bouts
of carpentry.

The Carpenter

My father says, you cannot tell
the true metal, it is mixed in this world;
he says, let's make a pact to talk to the dead;
he says, you can't assess the system you're in
when you're in it;
he says, I'm tired of talking to all these spooks.

I crawl out from under the four directions,
to sit with him, on the arm of his recliner,
at a window that looks over a threading willow
to the sea;

we glimpse sails,
and my mother, in the square below,
swishing her skirts against her stockings.

Skirts

You pull my sweater
over my head,
unbutton my kilt,
slip off the pin.

Pajama top,
then bottom,
teeth brushed,
and prayers.

You sit on the bed
and I pleat your skirt
with my fingers;
your kisses pattern my face
like a constellation.

I turn my face toward time:
you step backward, out-of-bounds.

My father and I peer through the fog
that undoes you, feet to eyes,

strands of hair, maybe a ring:

he looks at me, finds you there
as I ready him
trousers, shirt, socks, underwear,
pajama top and bottom
for bed.

Good night
Good night

Here it is.

Once

> My friend tells me her dream and I listen fully.
> About her son and daughter picking flowers.
> They look like little marmots—first, the flowers
> and then the children. It is a dream of marmots.
> —P. K. Page, "Marmots," *Collected Poems, Volume II*

Once, long ago the trees were frozen,
dull winter lowered, there were no flowers or choirs; my mother
still lived—yet the weight of grief, like a sack dully
hoarded, an armful of sad thought and mind
boarded over my eyes. I was an animal
kept warm, but why? Then light bleached the bed,
I sat up from my coffin—
My friend tells me her dream and I listen fully.

Ten dark-robed men stood nearby:
their presence surprised, like the earth mined,
or mountains gullied by time,
ten times the sharp incline and decline of the road.
One helped me step out,
and I stood, in my nightdress, the cold like a shower,
and the coffin folded like a suitcase on a dusty plain;
then the men left for the glacier points, perhaps to cave
or star or even higher.
They'd left her, not with food or water, but a memory—
about her son and daughter picking flowers.

I stood in a bowl of sand with seeds scattered among stones,
mountains on the far rim;
my hands searched the grains,

but change brought tears—and so the watered seeds awakened
until the grey alluvia bloomed,
grass hid the prairie in wind.
I gathered the hum of shortened shadows,
the petal's face, the turn of hours,
the bees' rhyme from asphodel to zinnia.
I counted fern-traced stones, sought
the touch of green, its smell…
Sometimes I spied the spill of contents
from that abandoned coffin, left to rot: stained plate and cup,
a faded garment—
then forgot as small animals, born to delight, stirred and crept.
They look like little marmots—first, the flowers
and then the children. It is a dream of marmots.

Then I crept from that rich garden
and stood at the mountain limit, my eyes ached at the sky
and opened to a glimpse of heaven,
an unstitch to every stitch, a Penelope's longing.

My children swam through fields of colours,
the marmots slid within their burrows:
world's evolution scryed their brains
and my children's children.

When I awakened then, there was no more sorrow in me
than the next breath of the unknown.

The Stars

God is the One who has set out for you, the stars,
that you may guide yourself by them
through the darkness of the land and of the sea.
We have detailed the signs for people who know.
—Sura 6, Verse 97, Qur'an

Once, when I lay awake in the morning,
the electrical sun igniting green
from the tall firs—
before the day I saw a tree stand still in the wind,
other trees' branches weaving sharp as forks and pins around it,
its trunk a spear carrying the ochre sky;
before I saw a thrush land in the burnt grass
and fall dead, its wings and tail spread flat,
beak, breast, heart stilled,
and time passed, enough for me to call my daughter, drink coffee,
wonder why
nearby birds kept on with their beak-digging, foot-hopping—
and then the thrush sprang up, resurrected—
before all that, that one bright original morning—

I saw my life in a hive, and it spun through its figure eights,
its flower skimming, its constant alighting with others—
I saw its path within that brimming whole,
the preordained, if you like, honey-making episode—
as necessary,
for it described a minute packet of time and space—
the same way, you might say,
God is the One who has set out for you, the stars.

Perhaps I have said too much, done too much
in my busyness; but the hive is one thing,
and my heart, broken by understanding,
is another: it fluctuates against my chest wall,
it transcribes a tide
of inner and outer: it turns its love toward its loss—
and yearns for the touch of my mother's heart—heartfelt
graze of her fingers, tentative trembling
arms, eyes green as a winter's tale:

loss will finish me
and yet
I dream a woman, not her, who points out a square
of stars, four-square, like the foundation of all,
as if I knew the world better than I realize,
from stem to stern, could name those stars, call them friend,
navigate wilderness, say with certainty to others
that you may guide yourself by them.

The first chill weeks of September,
the stars eased from the forefront of sky:
a cooler breath suffused the atmosphere,
veiled the summer wandering. The price
of change? Hidden, but supposed
in the new quiet of bird and insect.

Still in the dark, I opened the door to the morning, let out the dog
who cowered beneath a stirring knot of wasps
wrapped to the porch light. They fled, at once, inside,
their whir and anger filled the hall:
then slowly, over days, they died
while my grief gathered,
through the darkness of the land and of the sea.

I'm recounting miracles, I guess,
private as the sound that sparked creation—
the hum of bees, the sough of wind that speaks
a single syllable. To stand outside the tangle
of thought and rest in surety a moment—
why name the angel?
It does its work the moment it awakes:
We have detailed the signs
for people who know.

Night Words

Argo Navis

It is a great ship, with a high stern,
a ragged circle of stars for a sail,
blown ever westward along the southern horizon
by dark nebulae of dust and cold gas.

The keel is hundreds of light-years distant,
the compass, broken by the Milky Way,
brightens and fades—faint now for decades.

Who now will guide it over the trackless deeps
and the underworld of its passage?—
the sun, our sun, moves ever away.

In the dream my dead child's hands
make finger shadows on the wall of night:
faint stars that signal home,
and despite all evidence,
that *here* is our refuge and our strength.

Coombe

A valley running up from the coast,
a basin, a bowl, a deep vessel,
a place to lie in tall grass,
held in your arms:

sheep run down upon us
like a spill of milk from the lip,

and the shadow speeds up one side
of the bowl, cold as iron,
claw cold;

day and night race away
like a stream over rocks,
with a joyful sound

time cupped,
like the earth cups
the hours of every day.

Our lives gather, a twist
of magic powder in a paper
that once set free,
could take us, say,
to a ship,

Navis means:

No-wise
None of us
No way
None of them

although they had the idea
that if you stepped out from a cliff
your foot stretched to the cradle of sky

you could fly.

Surprise Hussar

The most ordinary
of those you love
suddenly turns

and mounts a horse
you didn't know was there;

it is plumed, decorated with silver,
and while you attempt to decode the sight

(he is white-uniformed, splendid)—
you wonder who you are
to have thought you knew him
or his gifts.

Could you handle a sword
if it presented itself,
do you know how to ride?

Carambolo UFO

If it weren't for the night drive
along the hot road in the white car,
wheat, oranges, sand
all bled to ruts of sifted colour
in the headlights;

if I hadn't seen for myself
the road divide
and beneath the curved edges of its fall,

the treasure itself, with its windows of gold,
its high walls,

then the word dropped out of the night
from a white web
might not have caught
at my heart
as it did

and said "city" as well as
your arms, your chest, the wide hand
of your pelvis,
the crown of your eyes.

Yes, I'm a believer
as the car lifts, as in a movie,
on a band of light,
a whip-hand of heat,

and I've made it, or missed it,
that ship.

The Cat Project

Is the Divine Presence inside or outside the world?

It began with a cat in the desert
bringing the sun in its mouth,

the sun
burned its way
through charred skin,

obliterated the howled word.

Pain stirred the darkness:
gave it hunger
and a cry.

The earth
emerged raw, ready to be struck.

A woman with a cat's head,
or just a cat,

or a human who
was put to death

stands at a threshold,
invites us to please,
after you,
pass.

Out of a deep hole in the snow
flies a rat's tail.

Out of another deep hole—
a red fox.

Out of the third hole
rises Watch Dog:
he binds you
with a collar,

takes you for a walk.

The waters beneath the earth
flow into my emptiness.

You were reborn as an animal,

you felt no pain
when you were caught:

your paws became white.

Seven days after my death
I felt nothing.

I slide my rings
along your tail
while you are bathing.

You seduce me
with water
sprinkled on my face.

When rain falls
we consider the tree trunks
beneath the leaves.

The cat's name is Rain Cloud

At the time of the flood
God's cat killed a mouse,

its spirit sang the earth
out of existence,

almost.

The song emptied the eyes
of a woman,
released her milk.

Why?

When I kiss you,
you have my
soul

in front of the moonlight
in a paper sack,

ready weighted
with stones.

Under the ocean,
in the forest,
on the prairie,

in the desert, within a few miles of food,
lost, unfit for use,
sealed in a vase…
is a cat who went missing for three days,
and returned with a live falcon.

I opened my heart—
its navigable channels—
to Rain Cloud.

Is there a purpose to your life,
as a whole?

III

The Pink City

The Pink City

for Rita and in memory of J.R.

Snow was falling when I returned the books
to the library, closed the bank account,
drove to the minister's house down a dirt track covered
with ice. The house was weatherworn, unpainted,
set behind a mesh fence within a garden of frozen weeds,

the curtains at the window
slithered aside
as I climbed the front steps.

A sense of pause before the door opened; a thin hard-faced man
in stained cotton
trousers and shirt, a loose blue cardigan, gave me
the plane ticket:

"Don't forget to phone your parents,
remember you'll have to send all that stuff home,
you can't expect to leave it here forever in your car.
You're not in trouble, are you?"

He takes off his slippers but, even bending, keeps
his eyes on me.

Trees, thin as starved children, stagger up the riverbank.
A motel, cream-coloured, shapeless, with a beer parlour
tacked onto one end, then a blob of pink, a drive-in restaurant,
and we draw up to the airport passenger lounge.
I give him my car keys, he helps me check in.
"Do you want me to wait? I'd promised I'd see you on the plane."

He coughs and wipes sweat from his yellow skin, his forehead
juts out, the eyebrows brown circumflexes over
deeply set blue eyes.
"You've enough money?"
Yes, I'm fine.

"About the car."
I'll let you know.

"Well," he says, his hands shoot out of his pockets, fly
onto my head, "the Lord's blessing on you." He steps away
and the automatic doors close
behind him.

On a red vinyl couch,
beside a desk, a guard,
a nurse who holds a paper cup
of the seeds Penelope swallowed:

Welcome to the circle of intimates, says Andrei.

Love?

Then:

Love is
a new dress,
thigh-high boots.

I wait,
talk poetry with George,
think of a dark room,
a red candle,
the slide of an old girlfriend
left on the bureau for me
to find.

Her black lace bra
and pants.

But the hook is deep
my heart never so whole
as when lurching on a leash, plunging
the whole way
for the first time.

Now:

"So, tell me, how you're feeling?"
He's a lean, gaunt-faced doctor in a black suit,
yellow skin and eyes,
a stethoscope around his neck.
I feel nothing.

"Are you unhappy?"
I take his hand and put it on my face
next to my mouth.
Here…I move the hand
to my eyes…here…I feel nothing.

"Close your eyes," he says. "Tell me when you feel."
The pin jabs my arm.

You don't understand.
It's only my face, and

who I am.

For Joy:

Are you still in pain?
Do you imagine at night
when you undress at the window,
that he will return the children?
Your heart, to him, is the shape of a coffin:
he has the key.

You look out at the trees—
every song is there,
each breath, the slippage of bone
inside you:
how long before you know
he is the enemy?

The farther that I climbed the height,
the less I seemed to understand.
—St. John of the Cross

The nurses in their jeans
smell like fresh snow.

The patients—only the "bad ones" wear pajamas—
watch TV,
cast spells of warm air with a lift of their hands.
These are the webs they live in.
Living vertically, says Andrei, *is a bore.*

My nurse is small,
in an overall and sweatshirt,
hair pulled back in a ponytail,
her task, she says, is to "establish contact."

Ask her how her orbit
paints the walls,
ask her about the tears
nailed to my eyeballs,
ask her
about the food on the plate
when she leaves me in the cafeteria—
green beans like tadpoles
swim to mashed potatoes.

Two women at the table—
one prefers not to speak—
the other, a Shakespearean scholar,
cut her hair, got fat, was sent by her husband for treatment.
"It's the plight of never being trained
to the sword," she says.

So, what are they doing to help?
"I eat pills, next week I'm getting ECT. It's wrong
to be depressed. Moral truth is an awning
over a dull street."

The horizontal essence of women
floats before me.

"At least I'm not as bad off as her,"
says Ms. Shakespeare of a red-haired woman
at the next table. "She's an alcoholic, and if she can't quit,
she'll die. I'm not going to die of being sad.

Am I?"

Pillars of fire by day and night—but
someone is beating a woman, and
tell me, why is the table of philosophy
set here on 3-B?

Seven a.m. shower (razor kept
locked at the desk), dress, walk the breakfast line, coffee,
slippers under heels, blouse cuffs stained. The night still has its knots
round us, long threads of sticky terror that lead back to beds,
under beds,
our human silence;
weak snuffles of us sucking up cereal.

I stretch in "the screaming room"—it is carpeted, soundproof,
empty except for mattresses and plastic clubs—
because this is what you do, during intermission,
before the main event,
because he doesn't yet know where to find you.

Doctor's orders:
do not imagine

do not procrastinate
do not do what you did before.

My mother is faithful,
visits each night,
her knitting in her bag,
fresh nightgowns, new socks,
her cheeks drawn in—
that trip up the elevator from the ground floor
begins with my birth,

but she doesn't know
what she thinks she knows,

says, "I've heard from him."
You didn't tell him where I was!

She looks away.
You couldn't have told him?

"It's only right that he should know."

She doesn't know what I don't tell.
That the miracle of escape
is an eggshell.

"We decided we should send him
his fare home. After all…"
She examines her gloves.
My head rolls back, my neck
a wet paper tube.

Four a.m. A telephone call.
By breakfast, three telegrams.
And a phone number.
And a time by which I have to call
or he will have killed himself and
everyone I know in Fredericton.
(How I wanted to tell
before he left for work,
say finish it now, kill us both,
but stopped my mouth,
somehow.)

I am not just the fly on the glass
a reflection
riddled with holes for mouth, eyes, ears,
throat.

When I can talk, I say, *One is lucky, indeed,*
to have no heart.

Portraits:

Teenage boy, son of important hotelier,
pulls blue thread balls from the tufts
of his terry robe, moistens them in his mouth,
flicks them with his fingers to the ceiling tiles.
Where they stick—over an area of about six square feet—
is the haze of a summer sky.

An old woman tied to a wheelchair weeps.
Another woman, Cora, middle-aged,

big, with a grey crew cut, sits beside her but cannot
summon a nurse because, after ECT, her speech is
a logged hard surface through which she scrapes.
I touch her hand. It's all right, I'll get someone.
She has been kind to me, and to Jesse, our roommate,
who does not sleep at night because people
pluck off her bedclothes and feed her cancer.

Jos is undergoing "primal,"
holds her black-haired baby under an arm.
Her husband, on the ward below,
comes for visits.
His eyes and the baby's eyes are plumbed dark pits.
Every day Jos looks better
as she retreats toward *her* birth.

Karl, blond, muscular, fit, almost never speaks,
smashes his fists into the piano keyboard.
He tries to play, but chaos crosses the notes.
I hear, inside the web of fatal noise a Beethoven concerto.
His favourite record is Paul Twitchell singing "All Is Love."

Raymond, English, a jeweller, draws diagrams to show me
the geometric workings of the world. Four colours
on each chart, all angles considered. A full notebook.
What about Yeats? I ask.
We discuss gyres, the Great Year.
He is about to be deported.
Hitchhiked across Canada, asylum to asylum,
to save money.
Scuttling along on his snow chains.

A girl who lived on the streets: thin eyebrows, a face like a pan
of skimmed milk. Finger-mark bruises on her upper arms,
slash marks on her wrists. The police beat her
when she tried to resist.
(Fourteen, at most.)

New on the ward: young thin woman, Colleen, with straw-blond hair,
face squashed on one side. Accompanied by boyfriend:
limp-haired, thirty, flare jeans, red string tie, checked shirt, cowboy
boots. He helps her hang up short flowered dresses,
put away pairs of white high-heeled shoes; she repairs her lipstick
before and after kissing him goodbye.

When he's gone, she shows us where he cut her with a bottle,
scars the blond peek-a-boo hair
hides.
She has just lost a baby, is depressed, and
occasionally violent. He does not
like noisy women, I hear boyfriend tell Bertha,

a nurse with fear-ambered eyes,
Bertha checks the wastebaskets for drugs,
reads our diaries, poems,
never looks
at us.

In the recreation room, Colleen removes "All Is Love"
from the turntable, puts on Tammy Wynette.
Karl, the pianist, comes in, the lights dim
I leave as she begins to have him on the sofa.

All is love,
and the urge to kill like the urge to begat,
puts on its boots and jacket.

Hunting the Hare:

Raymond, the jeweller, sits beside me on the couch.
I am waiting for my mother.
We watch the elevator.
Under cover of drawing more
diagrams, he scribbles his
escape plan. Immigration is coming
in the morning to deport him...

Problem: he has no clothes,
only pajamas, a dressing gown, and paper
slippers.
Solution: ignore problem.
He winks at me before
writing
Problem two: getting into the elevator away
from the scrutiny of nurses,
and once in the lobby slipping past the commissionaire.
Solution: go at visiting hours when patients sometimes
accompany visitors to the bottom floor and, anyway,
all dangerous patients are locked away, they won't care
(that much) about him.

Problem three:
once outside where to go in PJs?
Solution: Jos has a friend who lives nearby.

He will wait at the bottom of the steps in his car.
Ray will stay with him until Jos
gets out and after that maybe they
will live together, fall in love, make good parents for the
black-haired baby,
return to the cabin she left?

Her Story:

Up north,
beyond Bella Bella and Bella Coola,
in the forest, at the bottom of a valley,
on top of a mountain,
in a cabin around which wolves
howled all winter,
and snow bowled nightly at the door,
a baby was born.

A man, thin and cold,
elbows out of sweater,
eyes the lost blue
of the aurora borealis but
bad at chopping wood,
finds that fair skin retains his imprint
in a way the land won't.

Late at night
like an angel or a singer
he transforms
becomes an actor
or a soldier denied utterance

on a battlefield: his fists
speak of him, sound the note of life:
she wails, the infant, too
into the dumb frozen air.

One morning she wraps the child in fur,
wades through snowdrifts
down the mountain, across the valley,
and through the forest

to the nearest telephone. How many miles?
More than he thought she could walk when he beat her.
Help me. *The air is shivered by human cries.*
For a second only, while it lasted,
nature is all wonder, all silence.

Bertha is coming. "Ray!"
Ray eats the paper.

1. The elevator doors open and my mother,
straining her tired face into a smile,
gets out, carrying my laundry.
She sits beside me, kisses my cheek,
and nods at Ray. Ray takes another piece of paper
and sketches the elevator: the up/down button is given
prominence. He concentrates.

2. Bertha strides toward the recreation room.

My mother's voice, discouraged and remote,
is drowned out by shouts.

Orderlies flash by like fleet deer.
Bertha, flushed and excited, runs back to the nurses' desk,
returns with a long syringe in her hand,
her cap askew, on her cheek a scratch the colour
of Colleen's lipstick.

"You sons of bitches, cunts, whores, bastards!"
Patients and visitors lower their newspapers or books,
stop talking and gaze with mild interest.
Someone turns the television down. Karl, the pianist,
is led weeping to his room. His body seems
jumbled, its pieces out of sequence and shape, shattered
within the prison of his skin.
(Oh, and not so long after, the day he is released,
he steps from the pavement in front of a bus and is killed
in an instant.)

Colleen, corn-dolly hair standing up like thatch,
is wrestled to the ground. Her pretty dress, ablaze with peonies,
screws up around her waist.
Bertha yanks her panties down and jabs in the needle.
With a last effort, Colleen frees a foot from an orderly's hand and
kicks off a stiletto heel that strikes Bertha in the eye,
then, limp as a melted candle, she is carried
through a swiftly unlocked door marked INTENSIVE CARE.

3. "They said I shouldn't withhold anything from you
I'd tell you normally," says my mother.
The baby starts to cry. I pick him up and give him to her.
She has him quieted and sleeping in a few moments.
Bertha notices and takes the baby away. The baby wakes and screams.

Jos emerges from primal, at a run, to rescue him.
"I knew it would be you!" she cries to Bertha.
"They shouldn't let you have it here.
It's a crime to have a baby in a place like this!"
Bertha rattles her keys, retreats behind the desk.

My mother pulls a newspaper clipping from her handbag.
She says, as she gives it to me, "I wasn't sure,
but it sounded like somebody
you'd told me about who'd gone
missing."

Woman's body found in river.

Bludgeoned to death,
unsuccessful attempt made to hack
her head from her body,
dumped beneath the bridge,
may have been killed in riverside park,
reports of a woman's screams heard late at night.

That last night,
a night and a day remaining,
clouds tumbled over the hills behind the town,
mist rose from the river
and settled at the height of the bridge.
I thought I would search for the place
the poets were buried
across the river. There is no "why"

there were *ghostly strangers in the dark*
whose kisses scald and stay.

I started the car
and his head appeared at the passenger window.
"I wondered when you'd be going out," he said.

Were you watching for me to leave? His damp clothing,
and red hands and face pinched with cold, answered.
I drove through the tree-softened streets.
People scurried round corners toward their homes
as snow began to fall. I edged across the narrow bridge
and through the suburb. He kept on asking,
"Where were you really going,
what would you have done if I hadn't come along?"
So I decided to stop, so we could walk and maybe talk, and…

in a riverside park I opened the car door.
His hands went round my neck and pressed my throat.
I lay on the snow-spattered grass. The river was black
glass, the mist drawn into the sky. I could see streetlight
wands, the shimmering lace of headlights and windows
on the other side. I heard a cry come from the water,
but it must have been me, because he led me back and took the keys
and drove, reached over to pat and comfort, huge wet
rolling tears ran from his beautiful eyes.

The house, with its broken front window, took us in.
He pulled me up the stairs, put me on the bed,
reached under the mattress, a raft in a dark ocean,
and brought out a rope, tied my feet, wrapped it round my legs,
left for a moment, and returned with the rifle.

He bade me goodbye.
Then prayer like blood spurted from my mouth,
stopped him with its flood.

A graveyard hand travels my flesh.
"He arrived last night," says my mother. "He came to the house
last night.
He asked us to let you go. He seems to think
it's our fault."

She is weeping. I cradle her in my arms.
It's all right. Everything's going to be all
right.

Why put it in words? We're deep
into something else,
flames of cigarette lights,
tongues of sheep dogs.

I watch Ray make his way toward the elevator.
The door opens and disgorges two nurses.
Ray pulls at a thread end of his dressing-gown tie,
enters, holds the door, while I help my mother
inside with him.
The doors close and they
drop away into freedom.

October 31:

John, my old friend, and I
used to talk

about his life

above the sea
at the mouth of
a cave in Crete.

I slipped his worry beads
through my fingers
the night we walked all the way down
Alma from the UBC dance and sat, over coffee,
and he told me about the time, as a child, he believed
he'd been left behind in the Rapture, spent days, alone
in the woods, abandoned by God.

(When I lived, later, in Greece,
I used to see him like a dream, like the vapour
that streams from an icebox,
when I walked the chamomile- and thyme-scented hills.)

He was *careless about tomorrow,*
travelling light.
We had terrors, not love, in common
rippling deep
through the fir-tree gaps.

Raised, both, on fear of
eternal damnation,
we'd crawled
from the shadows toward iridescence:

but the brain is human
and the sensations peculiar to it,

the mischief of ice-pick assaults
on the spirit,

ring at a finger's touch:
so, one day, not now, I will write the story
of his exile, but now, this night
I gaze out the window of 3B and think
of his work in the school
at Alkalai Lake, his compact, silver blond goodness:

fireworks glow and then the splash
as a boat tips in the lake—
his friend is drowning—
sounds travel
much more slowly than light.

What does John think, standing on the shore,
the metal of courage in his mouth,
in the moment before his death,
is he back at the cave mouth
gathering courage for the leap
from the cliff
into blue water shirred by dolphins?

No time at all, perhaps, to imagine a consequence as
he leaps into *who we are,*
his heart staggered by cold water
into eclipse:
one's voice won't carry far in the heavy air:
when the snow lifts how brilliant,
how rare.

The clock says 2:30 a.m.
Jesse pulls the blankets
from my bed, wakes me, says I had stolen them.
Cora and I settle her in,
then I take a blanket and with the night nurse's
permission
sleep on the floor
of the screaming room.

In my dream, in my grief,
John brings a small white horse.
We ride her up a green hill.
"I am not dead," the horse that carries us says.
I dismount at the top
and watch it run
into the blue distance of its strange country
with my friend.

Before dawn I touch my eyelids and lips, feel the imprints
of my fingertips.
A white-faced clock clicks through several minutes.
And so, I've left numbness.

Glass curtains over the windows,
footsteps in the
corridors:
at the nurse's station someone works by lamplight
on patient reports.

Dreary cellars of our buried life!
Shall we attack these pictures with a knife?

The women, the men, desperate
to touch the green mist—
Not for us the song of the gas stove,
let the telephone ring it's not for us.

Note: The passages in italics are by Andrei Voznesensky.

IV

Glen Lochay Diary

Glen Lochay Diary

6 July/77

Dear Derek (and your wife, Joan) King:
I enjoyed my visit to the Whyte Harte Hotel in Bletchingley, Surrey.
I was jet-lagged, and worried,
meeting my lover after
a long absence.
I wore my lucky T-shirt and a new skirt, and carried my leather
trench coat. (It was a gift
from my mother; it has already crossed Europe.)
I am writing to say I left my white bikini
in Bletchingley.
You may remember speaking to me
at 5:00 a.m. in the hallway. You wore pajamas.
The bikini was my favourite,
with white lace and a little black ribbon
running through the top and at the waist.

Michael brought a bottle of wine from the Highland Show,
and two glasses; we'd driven from the airport down hedged lanes
in a green sports car. There was cool laced sun then bright light
when we turned into your courtyard.
The earth smelled of straw. You were busy in the bar…
We spent five pounds sterling to stay overnight.

(I could have walked the corridor in my underwear,
but I dressed, just for people like you—old,
censorious…)

When the servant brought tea at 7:00 a.m.,
I forgave the establishment.
If you find my bikini, please send it.

20 July/77

Moving into Tighnacraig (Rose Cottage), Glen Lochay,
near Killin, which is at one end of Glen Dockart by Loch Tay.

The nearest neighbour is Rob Cairns; the landlords are the Stroyans.
Angus Stroyan passes the cottage wearing a yellow pesticide backpack,
spraying nettles. "Have you got a dog?" he shouts.
"No."
"Well, there's one after a roe up in the hills. It's not yours?"
(He wipes his forehead.)
"Would you like a cup of tea, or a beer?"
"I could do with one…but I haven't time."

He's sorry he isn't acquainted with my work.
He asks for a copy of a book.
He's a judge down in Yorkshire.
Angus Stroyan of the nettles.

I write upstairs in my little room,
I cook venison, make bread.
In what's left of a garden are red currant bushes,
blackberry canes, the remains of a spinach patch.
Swallows nest in two sheds behind the house,
sheep stare through the fence.
When the sun goes down, very late,
the hills are black.

Tonight there's a house-warming,
Phil brings me foxglove as a present.

I've lost track of time, but I want them gone,
want our room, our bed,
you.

27 July/77

Phil drives the van to the head
of the glen, opens the gate
to Glen Lyon with a key
(where does one get such a key?).

We lean forward
into the weak headlights

but can't read the road:

there's a dark arm of wet pavement
and the pale scar of the dam—

Bob Bissett, the shepherd,
lives to the side of it.

Inside, a peat fire smokes,
we drink whisky;
handmade shoes and violins
hang on the wall.

He tells of riders around him
in the hills,

in the heather, at night,
horses screaming,
blood on the swords.

I'm half awake in the stinging smoke,
where there are no ghosts.

Time is a pool
of rain and dust,
you have only to touch it
with your lips.

There's a cold wind
from the north,
someone with wet shoes,
all that's solid,
almost enough.

29 Sept/77

Out of the slurry of red puppies
in a Dunfermline kitchen
we pull Grainne:

she sits on my lap
on the long drive home.

It is dark, raining,
cold wind slithers
through the MG soft top.

There's no snow yet,
we're in a painting
of brown and grey rock,
a pewter stream and sodden light;
the road hugs the hillsides. General Wade's abandoned bridge
links stream banks far below, pale deer flee.
The car is a rolling can of nails,

everything's broken
but the power of stone,
charms against dying,
and the fist of sleet that
slams us.

You write in my journal, so I'll remember: Drive carefully—
remember you're on the left. If you're lost, ask.
I love you.

(Here's the route by Glen Devon:
from Kincardine Bridge to Yetts o' Muchart,
right at Drum, bear left at Stirling signs,
follow Crieff signs, right and right again;
then through Glen Devon, Muthil, etc.;
at Crieff follow the signs to Crianlarich…)

4 Oct/77

You take the puppy
all the way into Killin—
past the hydro station, over the hump
where the sheep gather in the dark—
to get the car.

Dochay's replaced the Hardy-Spicer joint,
aligned the wheels, put on new brake pads.
You and Grainne visit the dairy, the butcher,
the post office.
If I'd gone, I'd stop
at the mill to see Celia, ask her
to open the iron grille
to the niche in the wall
where St. Fillan's stones nest
in a bed of straw and reeds
washed down the Dochart.

Woollen hats and gloves, lambs' wool sweaters,
gentlemen's scarves and toy sheep,
key chains, postcards, Robbie Burns's trays
for the tourists…

When Celia opened the grille, I'd take the stones
and hold them in my palms, rub Aunt Daisy's hankie over them.

(Celia wears the key round her neck.
She lives with her mother over the bakery.
Just once she's walked out to the cottage to see me.)

You're home with the car:
your hands cup the puppy,
the wind from Craig Cailliach blows from the west,
lifts your hair. Behind you is the new byre,
back of that, the hill,
the trees, bareness.

5 Oct/77

Buy wellies, stamps, milk, and groceries.
Vacuum, pulling a cannister of noise over the carpet,
circulate the dust.

You take the dog up the hill
to the old shieling.

Walk to the pub in the evening.

The dog and the cat follow us,
the puppy at heel, the cat a shadow
as she slips from tree to tree
along the ditch. At the last moment, as we near
the lights, she jumps into my arms, dives into the pocket
of the big beaver-lamb coat Margaret's lent me
for the winter.
Ride back with Rob and Betty,
climb the attic stairs,
hole with both hands to the rails.

6 Oct/77

Walk to Daldravig, across the river and up to the power station.
Mr. MacTaggart, the factor, can supply us with a couch,
new cooker, a fridge. The wind comes from the east,
brings rain showers and cold.

I read you to sleep:
Narnia, George MacDonald Fraser, poems.

Lights turned off: kerosene lamps blown out,
the coal fire flickers and dies.
Under the duvet I wear sweaters and socks:
your long feet tuck up under my thighs.

After midnight Grainne rises from her blanket
in the kitchen, pads into the front room,
noses the cat, Solon, awake.

How does it start? Is it the moonlight
crossing the floor, or the ghosts who travel
the road, the moan of cattle
in the byre opposite?

Solon stretches, arches her back, leaps onto the
sideboard, and they're off,
over the couch and chairs, round the
dining table, a rattle of moonlight
at their heels.

You swear, throw off the covers—
they screech to a stop: two innocents
licking coats smooth in the torch light.

"You're freezing!" I say as you come back
to bed, I try not to laugh—you're so cross.
The animals hold their breath—I can hear
them listen as you begin to snore,

then I listen no more.

14 Oct/77

Stew and Margaret up:
we put in time with a ride
to Firbush—the wind whips
the stony loch edge, flattens the sails
of the Wayfarers.

It's the night
of the Mountain Rescue dance
at Lochearnhead Hotel—

Rob and Betty, Dochy and Rosie,
and Donald troop by.

Behind the closed
ballroom door—
reels and strathspeys,
the mysteries of *settes,*
pas de bas, the jounce of accordion:
everyone (as they slip in)
has a smile for us, sitting at the bar,
and then a slight
down-turned eye
as they see
no dancing shoes
or kilts,
no broad sashes
or *skian dubhs*
on us
but
drinking too much
anyway.

17 Oct/77

There's a road, back up the glen,
above the power station: we park at the top,
walk over peat, heather, bog myrtle,
bog laurel, bog cotton, higher than the ledge
where we watched the gathering in the summer
and the sheep ran in white rivulets.

We cross the burn, up the rocks to
the summer shieling; higher still to lie under
the wind. When I open my eyes,
three red deer are poised, antlers tipped, curious to see
how I've shaped your head, your thighs.

28 Oct/77

Trouble lighting the fire.
Read. Walk to the Falls of Lochay

6 Nov/77

A *dreich* day. Low cloud on Tarmachan,
thick cloud on broken country
of Craig Cailliach. Hill walkers
disappear over the back to the quarry.

In the late afternoon we drive to Edinburgh.
Stewart is in hospital. He is afraid
of the doctors and nurses; he wants to go home.

It's a conspiracy; the drugs are poison.
He's right:
dying is madness—
tea on carts, crepe-soled shoes, the flip of charts,

a few drinks afterward in the pub.

11 Nov/77

For four days I've marinated pork
in white wine, pepper, cloves, onions, thyme, and bay.
I'm a poet who never thought she'd have to cook
for a prospective father-in-law.
The only recipe I know is for roast
boar.

Two pounds of good chestnuts,
boiled in water with fennel,
keep hot on the stove.
I put coal on the fire, let the dog in,
check for dead rabbits in the yard,
walk between the rowans
at the front gate.

The green MG tops the little hill:
Stan, Michael's dad, uncurls,
helps Michael bring the groceries in.

I serve the plate of bones: "What am I meant to
do with these?" Stan says, stirring them.

Out the back door and follow the burn
up the hill; clear grass and dead mice
from the water intake pipe;
keep walking, sheep kicking
like spray from my heels;

climb, with a stone in my hand
for the cairn.

12 Nov/77

We go for a walk,
pass Rob's farm—Daldravaig, the "Field of the Slut"—
past the white bridge and the black bull.
Stan's black oxfords
are wet from the turf.

On the way home watch the Lochay flow:
tourmaline water and darting fish. Something slow
has its fingers in gravel,
mouth wide, open throat.

Here are the landmarks:
a circle of beech in the drowned field,
three bulls—black, red, and white—
silver coins tossed into the water, silver stones,
silver light.

We cross—my boots, Stan's smooth soles,
Michael's feet in runners—
my heart is hammered to metal.

If I were there now, I would say, hold my hands,
both of you, I won't let go.

15 Nov/77

Shit in the kitchen.
Margaret skids across the floor.
The dog hides.
We yawn awake,
Kojo, the parrot, coughs Stewart's cough
as we sit, with the paper, in two rocking chairs
at the gas fire. Margaret puts out a cigarette
and cooks breakfast.

Was somebody crying in the night?
I hear it in motels and hotels, in the homes of
strangers: but this is the morning of the funeral in Margaret's house.

I dress in jeans and sweater, take the yellow mini to Blackhall
with my list: four bottles of MacKay's, two Famous Grouse,
gin, sherry, beer.

Who does the housework? Who puts out glasses, napkins,
makes sandwiches? I only remember trays of ice,
and wearing the heavy beaver-lamb over a dress.
There's a crowd at the "cremie": we're all right
until the coffin slides away,
the curtain closes, end of play.
We hurry to the car: but there's Barb from Ireland
and Hildegarde…and
all the old guard come back to the house.

Someone on a diet sips coffee on the sun porch.
I sit in Stewart's study, in his chair: on the wall
is a painted map of Africa and the frayed hide of a zebra.

That land far away.

To Meadowbank to watch Edinburgh lose to the Anglo-Scots
at rugby: why do we go?

A soul is watching the house, the bedroom, Margaret
in her heels and dress covering Kojo's cage. Good night, says the parrot in
Stew's voice. Good night. Good night. Sweet good night.

16 Nov/77

We'll go home soon, but first climb Arthur's Seat.
Thick mist and cloud: boots slip. You give me your
hand. Who do I see ? Not the ghost of anyone I know
but ghosts, all right, and horses,
and cars pursuing their headlights
over the cliff.

18 Nov/77

A cold day. The chocolate spread's frozen.
Drinks yesterday at the pub; today you're at the Ardeonag hotel.
Not me—
I'm at home writing my will.

Gloves on, wrapped
in a blanket, the dog and cat at my feet.
I leave you my ring and the years until I lose it.
I leave my sweater and the new long kilt you will give me at Christmas.
I leave your mother's old coat, my Frye boots, my vest,
a sheaf of new poems and all the drafts…

I leave you the hills
and the threshold of Tighnacraig,
the icy burn that supplies our water,
my wet socks, a cracked teapot,
frozen milk
tinned milk, and the sugar in the pantry;
letters, beginning and ending with love;
our tangling through layers of cloth.

Two gin bottles of water taken from St. Fillan's well,
said to cure madness.

21 Nov/77

Gears gone in the MG: drive all the way to Edinburgh in third.

22 Nov/77

Strange to sleep alone
in the nursing home.
I get out of bed, gaze down
at the wet street and
three women and two men in the road,
lift the sash, cry "Hello!"

The crepe-soled anesthetist
enters at midnight,
breathes whisky into my nose
holds my hand, weaves his way home—

they drug the Ovaltine.

I lose you in my dreams:
you are wringing out red hands:
oh, the sadness.

And where are you? In the scrap yard, and the motor pool,
wrestling with the clutch and flywheel.
My surgery ticks past, out of your grasp.
I end up
fine
on the couch at Margaret's, watching the coal fire
burn. Her hands hold a crystal glass's glint.
Sherry, diamonds, some human limit.

26 Nov/77

Ice and hard-packed snow on top of Ben Lawers
where you are.
I'm upstairs in Tighnacraig at my desk.

Then it's night, a fall of light from the window
onto the road;
inside later—a spill of hands and shadows.

The rowans scratch the gate shut.
A weight settles. It's dust to dust,
something like that,
or the first time I
bared my breasts: like that.

29 Nov/77

Stupid argument. Stupid. Stupid.

1 Dec/77

Ice in the peat bog
under your boots;
your hands are red with cold:
I can see your breath live
outside you, each word a white pause.

Cold.

8 Dec/77

We don't get any sun now,
the hill's too high.
In your dream your grandfather glides
from shadow to say he must return, at once, to his bed.
Did you call him? Don't you know he's dead?
In my dream we ride a red motorbike,
drop a hundred feet over a cliff

to a dirt track,
get away with it.

But where is the road through the hills,
the green road away?

24 Dec/77

We drive up the glen
to collect stones from the stream
to hold the Christmas tree in a bucket.
I pick rose hips and string them,
tie grouse feathers onto branches,
loop garlands of chestnuts. Margaret adds
fairy lights, holly from Moy's.

Rob rides by on Zian, stops for a stirrup cup—
a white horse for our star
this dark night.

26 Dec/77

To Raeburn place.
You show off your
Scotland Forever underpants—a present
from me. Fighting with me, and Margaret.

I write poems to stay awake, look out
onto the rugby field, drinks coming to the table
behind me. What's spoiled it?

That drunk boy who speaks to me soon dies.

29 Dec/77—2 Jan/78

The river is a tunnel,
the wind a rough hand
forcing you to sleep.

Awake! The hills drift snow
on the long deep frozen grass,
the edge of the moon is like a finger snap
of bone:

I was there, cold, my teeth ached,
my heart so full of light,
I was bringing it to you.

At Crianlarich the train is late:
it creeps into the station while we cup
frozen hands around mugs of tea
in the waiting room.
Its wheels creak through ice,
barely stops to let off Susan and Jeff.
They've two big suitcases. Susan wears an ancient coat,
Jeff blinks,

and they fall

into Hamish MacGregor's ancient rented car (the MG's too small).
We drive past St. Fillan's well where the mad are cured;

the road slides away into valley,
stones and small pines, the heartbreak, years on…

Wind and frost write on our faces,
sad traces more than sad.

Pheasant for dinner (left hanging on the door handle
by Neil, the gamekeeper);
the Famous Grouse, straight, from the bottle.

Nothing broken, that night.

At Shian's Moor:

In the air are the tones of wet fingers
on wet glass rims, the harmonies
of water, peat, sedge, lake,
a cup of bottomless grey sky.

Each bird is the last of its kind,
the earth here is the last bowl
on the last plate of the planet.

Nothing human moves
but our cold hands in our pockets. You could cry
for the weeping air, the moor of
silver, purple, russet; the browns
of rabbit, stoat, rat, vole; the malted feathers
of the golden eagle let fall: here might be
the spring we have sought, the thirst quencher,

heart-stopper: if we have the courage not to move,
say nothing, idle between the folds of the world.

No wonder that stillness,
in Hamish MacGregor's rented car, my hand
on yours on the gearshift.
At the Kenmore Hotel we drink hot toddies:
my golden friends, mist and feathers…

31 Dec/77

There's a little stream
where the branches catch,
and the mice swim:
Solon, the cat, crouches in a tree over it.

Sheep edge down the steepness,
their madness slithers, stops,
escapes in little runs.

1 Jan/78

On one of the few pages
to survive the fire of the green notebooks,
I've written several bars of music. A note falls
from Sron a Clachan; a question on the stone tiles
of the roof slips through the open skylight,
settles its feather motes on my hands
at the little green table where I write.

Downstairs, Grainne and Solon rearrange the furniture.
Bass clef G major—the house voice
in the chimney, coal and wood smoke,
mouse dung,
bird bones at the bottom of
the coal sack, cracked by the stoat.

I rub frost from the skylight:
there's the wing shape of the hill cleft,
behind it—sky, sugared with cloud.

Behind the first rise
is another, and another, then
cow bones at the cairn; our toy house
is silent.

30 July/99

New people on the road.
The same road, but the fields
are overgrown with bracken,
and Zian's gone,
Rob's gone from the farm.

There's a loose dog (where's Angus Stroyan when you need him?),
somebody else's car at the cottage,
the garden's run-down,
the fairy mound
is all long grass. No good crops,
no caretakers:

where have they gone, the good ones—
Celia, Dochy,

old Mrs. Stroyan? Gone under,
with Stan and Margaret
and the red deer that smashed
headlong
all autumn.

I throw in a coin at the small bridge:
remember me
hills and streams
in the glen of the Black Goddess
Glen Lochay.

(If I were there,
at the rowan trees,
at the gate, bending to touch
Grainne's neck, wearing Margaret's coat,
I would ask why it hurts
to look
at torn sky, its grey silk shredding,
and you, resting on a hillock, drinking tea,

a spell of weather
coming in.)

V

Calendar

January I

Pink

I ask to be taken
to the place
of the dead.

We go on a bus,
we get off at a fairground,
walk up and over a hill—
it is muddy and difficult.
At the top they point and say, "Here is
the pink city."

Below are flesh-coloured coffins,
thrown like pulled teeth,
or rubber erasers.

People are dancing.
My cousin, Sylvia, says,
"It is witchcraft."

"You have to keep cutting," I say.
I move my fingers like scissors, snipping
the threads they throw
to catch us.

I cut thread after looping thread.
A man cries,

but we are not trapped,

we are not dead,
we are not caught
in the pink city.

Orange

My father remembers a young girl
who died of her burns.
The kids were jumping
a bonfire. She was very little,
she tried to do the same,
and fell in.

It was his first funeral. There was a
horse-drawn hearse, and buggies.
The mother walked behind,
crying, *My Lala's gone.*

Yellow

I have two sweaters—the yellow one
that Stephen's mother made,
and the pink, with holes, from the Sally Ann.

I give them to my daughter,
who may have followed me

down the cold road
that sprang up
from the fairground.

January II

I meet the dead buying groceries.
They hurry their bags to their cars,
drive off before I can catch them.

Much colder today:
we wait for the hearse, follow it,
squealing round corners,
race through the streets of Guildford,
lose sight of it, catch up…

There's a backlog because of the holidays,
they're on a tight schedule…

It's January. People force themselves
on walks; their noses stream,
cows turn their backs.
At the end of a lane,
horses test the earth for hollows.

Reverend Strevens in his long black cloak
comes to bury you.
It's January. Through the lych-gate,
under the yew. We stand.
"What is dying? A ship sails and I stand watching…"

February I

February is for coats—secondhand coats.
In the seams of your blue tailored raincoat
I've sewn animal tails.

I put on the coat and go for a walk.
Branches fly past, the great trees toss their heads.
The earth is cold, the fires banked low.

When the storm comes—later, at night—
somewhere, inside a cave,
is a wall painting of a horse
and pictures of bison,
small deer, and dogs.
The colours are gold, red, ochre.
I am in the cave, painting, looking out at you
looking in at me,
and sewing a warm coat.

In the wind, while outside in your coat,
I met a ghost who had killed herself.
Her husband had murdered her lover;
she threw her children down a waterfall
near Tahsis.

She is distraught still.
I gave her the coat.
I came home wet.

February II

When I wear grief
like a helmet and armour,

when the horses are in the far field,
and the woods between are impassable,

I lie on the ground.
You have never seen me like this.

You would hear the horses and start walking,
look back at me with hate.

When I am done,
and my face is sour with salt,

I dream myself free
into my allowance of love,

let my grandmother lead me
into the forest

where I may never come out,
or find the horses,
or ride away,

though it is sweet
to remember her sweetness.

February Note

The world is dangerous.
The dead arrive at night to bring me presents:
(Dorothy Livesay's snuff box, for instance).

I forget I am married.
I have a lover with a red condom.

When my uncle went water-skiing,
at eighty, my aunt crouched in the bow of the boat,
praying.

Now he is ill: people are taking his money;
he cannot walk,
he is always running.

March

I remember Stan appearing to Xan in a dream—
she rose, brimming with joy,
to float above the bed before she fainted.

He'd slipped through the door,
his shoes were polished;
she knew it was him
by the Arrow shirts, the grey slacks—
he'd returned from the land of the dead.

He said all was forgotten,
except for the feeling of lunch in the apartment,
the red dust,

horse fleas biting his legs
as he rides
across a stream
into mountains.

April

April opens with snow:
my house, the trees,
the fall of land
to the lake, turn white.

When we see where we are,
we're flooded: water to the back steps
and inside over the floor.

Mr. Chalker appears in gum boots
and with buckets: we sweep water
away from coal sacks,
suitcases, books.

I go to bed (the window blank with
melting ice) and hold your sweater
to my face.

Somewhere, not many miles from here,
is a house. If I could find it,
the links of time would join.

Our room is there, a brass bedstead,
apples in the cellar,
our children, a grandmother:

my grandfather whips the little horse,
Forest, pulling the cutter—

we are cut off by the last
of spring snow.

When I walked to school,
I passed a wood
I called "Sad Crimes."

One time I stopped and went in:
branches shifted—

it was spring.
White petals
swam the air.
I did not have
a question,

so stayed silent
behind a tree,
while a man
took a shovel to wet humus,
tilled out a shining coil of worms.

Tonight I stand at the window,
young buds prick the maple,

but I see snow from that last storm
in St. John's when I stood,
with Mr. Chalker, broom in hand,

sweeping water
like a woman.

May

When they put me in the hospital,
I was Ophelia,
because Ophelia was mad,
and *her* lover had hurt *her*.

I understood Ophelia
when I looked up from my book
to see my lover open my blouse
with his knife.

I searched for her through boxes of books,
I looked through the town,
behind a church,
across a bridge
where lights stung the water,

and in a park
where my lover said,
Are you ready to find out
who you are?

When I was twelve, I went to the library.
The books spoke softly.
It was spring,
thin grass grew on the boulevard.

Next door was a sweet shop.
I went in and counted glass jars;
Ophelia stood on tiptoe in a dark room.

(When God tells you to do it,
you cross a bridge.)

June
for Jakob

Linda lived at the edge
of East London,
with a big wild hill
at the end of the street.

The wildness stopped
at an asylum. One day
a neighbour girl was grabbed
by a half-naked man,

but nothing happened.

Linda and I walk between hawthorn hedges,
buttercups and nettles blow,
the sheep, a Greek chorus, gather beneath an oak
to cry, *you can't have it all,*
it is never enough,
you can't stay here,
and if you do, you won't like it.

We watch our words,
tread softly along the mown path
between graves
at the end of the lane,

look down
at the rich brown water
of midsummer.

If you say the wrong thing, says Linda,
you'll end up dead.

I dream I am in the dark,
holding hands with Linda,
and others, in a chain.
I dream that somewhere
at the end of us
someone is made well.

July

A father hit golf balls
into a wire fence
and at black-headed gulls
and oyster catchers gathered
at the sewer outlet;

a child put clothes on and off;
a mother sat in the cold
and watched the power station
to the south.

Linda tramped north into the wind
to watch islands sink
and the estuary grow.

Then Linda wanted a drink,
so we drove for miles and took a road
and stopped on a square of gravel
in front of a house.

The house was closed,
but Linda hammered
on its great oak door.
Eddie opened it and said
it was unusual for people to knock
when the house was shut;

we'd woken him from his nap.

We sat near the window in the bar,
and Eddie, in deck shoes, paced in and out.

I began to weep
there, in the room across

from the long gallery,
beside the fireplace,
below the hidden hammer-beam ceiling
from the fifteenth century,
in a house first built in the twelfth century,
with a Norman dovecote nearby where there were once
two thousand doves;

I thought at first the house shook,
but it was me,
filled with whatever could not be contained,
like the arrowhead on an arrow
or the perpetual stream.

Eddie said
the house liked some people.
Linda remained polite while Eddie explained
that the house met five ley lines
and sheltered twelve spirits,
one of whom was an abbot who illustrated books.
And another was himself,
Prior Eddie.

I wept on
as the view included a moat,
and an orchard where I used to walk.

Eddie said
did I remember the romps we took
in the meadow with orchids underfoot?

He padded near in his deck shoes,
grinned, touched my hair,
leaned in for a kiss.

Linda said
it was time to go.

An oak steadied a field,
the forest was smoke

(and the sorrow I felt
on leaving the house
has remained:

no charm but the mystery of
accident
to keep us sane).

August
for PK

Mrs. Mary Watson of Holly Cottage
has to drag a small mattress in
from the caravan to sleep us:
she's a tiny hundred years old, with sharp eyes.

The downy and pillow are scented,
the bathroom sink's so small
I rinse one hand at a time
before I lie down.

Outside, are pale pink
and red roses, rhododendrons,
a stout box hedge:
beyond the hedge, a narrow road,
a pasture, forest and hills:

behind these
a stone-walled yard
in which a dozen huskies—
thousands of miles from home—
paw and howl.

Each afternoon
they run the track up Doon Hill:
the dogs are training for snow.

Black cows graze the hill,
slow as boulders
against the grey sky,

a grey-and-white cat sits
on an aggregate rock

to watch us palm
thumbnail-size golden frogs
that share the road with us.

Our feet strike hollows,
a pale green light
lays a wash
on the oak floor,
and the hollies and rowans
through which the huskies run.

At the top, under a pine,
letting the wheeled sled drop,
they lie down,
as did the Reverend Kirk
who vanished
the fourteenth of May 1692,

and who knew
that desire is a harmony
with loss,
and the unseen, like imagined sea or snow,
sustains a dream
so real we may find it.

Thin strips of paper tied to branches,
swing like tongues:

Dear fairies, I wish for my cousin to come alive,
I wish my family would be happy,
I wish you to care for Breaker. He was a great dog.

Wind shoves my back, pushing me to
the stony drop
of the fairy hill.

Mrs. Mary Watson smiles
when I recount
how I crawled on my knees
to the inner wood,
and the warm improbable breath of sled dogs
who ran as if they could smell the Arctic,

their hearts geared to the evidence
of the disappeared.

September

1.
My friends die in September.
They talk of grammatical structures,
and then they begin to sew new clothes.

There are two sides to a pause:
you would think they would remember—
like sunlight on water   or an empty house.

I dream I'm hanging from a porthole:
when the ship veers,
I am flung out—
if I can't hold on, I will die.

Those who *have* died find new life.
Their eyes touch my hands,
but they have no strength.

They don't know that the ship turned sharply;
they don't know about open portholes.

I am on one side of a caesura:
my feet are wet   I am so tired.

You would think they would recall
that all lost causes
end in September.

2.
I was glad it was over.

I remembered my father
sawing boards in his workshop.
I recalled the faithfulness of the bee
all summer: the hive,
the honey,

the last bee dance
on the windowsill.

October I

Perhaps it was autumn:
there was rain,
the door slammed;

the postman prowled
in a black rubber cape;

dark fell: we waited,
but it was daylight
when the pup hobbled home.

Our father said he was hit by a car—
and the street wore chrome
and a cruel eye.

That night I found the car,
wrenched the wheel from the driver,
killed him…

(And the moon
slipped under the granite roots
of islands,
lit them
like samples
of carpet snagged
on the seabed,
and
I named the colours—
as if they could be caught

skinking up a stairway
to a bright room.)

October II

Above the hearth,
before the shelves holding three books,

a small cupboard
is sketched in air—
only her eyes can open it.

It holds the spirits,
but on Saturday night
they come out.

They scent the room,
they trail through the debris
of hearts,
they examine the dead.

Her brother knocks
on their shared wall
at midnight.

He seems to say he is alive;
however, he may appear
in a room with parents,
on the walk to school,
or as he hunches his neck
over homework.

He seems to say remember that I am alive,
if I forget.

She opens the cupboard door again
just in case
there is anything else,

and there is.

November I

In her dream, while she is fainting from cold,
the child imagines a blackboard.
She draws a house, trees, a path, sunshine.
She is inside the house
eating pancakes.
She plays the piano,

sits on a beige carpet touching the lamp cord
softly to the socket.

Around her is a blanket of noise:
not the wind, not Lucifer filling her hollow bones

but the hiss of a swan,
its wings trembling fabulous air.

November II

The child shut in the cupboard
whispers the secrets of her life
to the coats. Their skirts bell,
their heavy folds remove her head
from her body.

When she is brave enough,
she tries the door—how many times
can she bear to find it locked?

Grit from boots and shoes
on her bare thighs,
her arms hug her knees:
do not feel sorry for her—

each coat has a voice
and two arms
with which to love her.

December

In December "every form that you see
has its original in the Divine world."
Death is of no consequence,
because there is eternity.

I bend my head to drink.
Timeless water drips from
my lips. It is no substitute,

it does not remember intelligence or faith,
it cannot recall you to me—you who have finished
with this world.

Pass into the deep, if you must,
so that the one drop which is yourself
may become a sea:

but do not drown,
put on your shoes,
set out as if to visit me.

Midnight
for Michael

There was snow thick as silver coins,
there was the silence
of broken windows.

The street was troubled
with the heels of the dead,
their broad calves
and trembling knees.

Their open mouths
swallowed our breath,
their wet hands touched my belly:
"Not here," I said,
and put down my suitcase.

The street stopped its wail
of wrongs,
the dead watched you kiss me,
take out the map,
say, "I'm sorry, I'll make it right."

They were pressed so close
I felt their ragged heartbeats,
the swoon of their longing
to be alive

and not dead
in the abandoned streets
in the dark below Sokolovska station
after midnight.

I saw the snow slide
from their black galoshes,
I saw the mud of the sewers
from which they'd climbed;

I was decades late,
but I had come
on the last train
from Vienna
to the city
at midnight.

I can still see the torn paper
of the snow,
feel the V of the roadway underfoot—

no one loved,
but rats fucked
on drainpipes,
on twisted bed frames,
in the wrenched doorways.

We climbed toward a light:
the dead clutched at my long coat,
my scarf, my heavy suitcase.
Their fingers tucked
into my buttonholes, they pulled,
but you held my hand

all the way to Sokolovska.
The soldier who came
could not help,

but the woman with him said,
"Help will come,
no harm will befall you,
it's Christmas night."

Acknowledgements

Epigraph (page ix): *Complete Works*. Vol. 1. Saint Teresa of Avila. Trans. and ed. E. Allison Peers. London: Sheed & Ward, 1946.

"The Alchemy of Happiness": *Out of Bounds* prison magazine, vol. 19, no. 4, for "The Stars."

"The Pink City": The Andrei passages in italics are taken from *Nostalgia for the Present*. Andrei Voznesensky. London: Oxford University Press, 1980.

"Calendar": *Exile* magazine for the majority of the poems in this section; for early versions of "February I," "April," "September," and "December," *Breaking the Surface*. Victoria, BC: Sono Nis Press, 2000.

MARILYN BOWERING has had two previous volumes of poetry nominated for the Governor General's Award: *Autobiography* and *The Sunday Before Winter*. The former also won the Pat Lowther Award. Her novel *Visible Worlds* received the Ethel Wilson Fiction Prize and was shortlisted for the prestigious Orange Prize. Bowering is also the author of *Human Bodies: New and Selected Poems* and the novel *To All Appearances a Lady*. She lives in Sooke, British Columbia.